Christmas

BabyKids™ books are designed for your child's learning and enjoyment.

Finding a Christmas Tree

Ornaments

Bells

Holly

Gingerbread Cookies

Candy Canes

Stockings

SANTA'S WORKSHOP

Santa Claus

Sleigh

Toys

Christmas Eve

Snow
Flakes

Snowman

This is Christmas Day.
Can you find:

1 Cookie
2 Stockings
3 Toys